Trivia For Kids:

Animals

By Elizabeth Gross

Introduction

This book of trivia facts is intended for children in grade school. The author is not an educator, so no level of ability is implied. Younger kids will enjoy learning new things, and older kids can show their knowledge. Adults can use the book as a teaching tool.

The animals are listed in alphabetical order to make finding a favorite easy. There is one animal for each letter of the alphabet. Each animal has a paragraph about it, ending with a multiple-choice question which is another trivia fact about the animal. Answers are found at the back of the book.

The title page art is by Alex Evans. All other illustrations are royalty-free taken from the internet.

Aardvark

The name for this mammal means "ground pig," but it is not a pig at all; it's an anteater. Aardvarks live in the southern part of Africa. It has sharp claws and long tongues that it uses to dig up ants and termites to munch on. An Aardvark is a big animals: 2 feet high and 4 feet long. It lives underground in burrows and is nocturnal. When chased by an enemy, like a lion, how do you think the aardvark tries to get away?

1. It runs in a zig-zag.
2. It shouts, "Get out of here you big, fat lion!"
3. It jumps into a river.

Bison

The bison is also called the American buffalo. It lives on the prairies of North America, eating grass while it wanders around for miles. A bison likes to wallow in the mud. This is to get rid of bugs and flies from its shaggy fur. Back in the 1800's, cowboys and Indians hunted the bison for its meat and fur. There are still many in the wild, but today most are kept on farms, just like cows. Bison are so famous in America they have a picture on something we use everyday. Can you guess what it is?

1. A can of soup
2. The bottom of your shoe
3. A nickel

Cassowary

A cassowary is a bird that kind of looks like a cross between an ostrich and a velociraptor. It's a bird that lives in the forest, but cannot fly. It has tiny wings, a large bony wedge on its head, and a bright blue neck. The Cassowary live in New Guinea and Australia, where it runs through the bushes. Its feet have very sharp claws which it uses to fight off enemies. A cassowary will eat something that helps it digest poisonous or bitter fruits. What do you think it is?

1. Soil (dirt)
2. Green leaves
3. Pickle juice

Dormouse

Dormice live in Europe where they make their home in woods and forests. They look like house mice, but have very bushy tails. Fruits, berries, flowers, and insects are a dormouse's choice of food. They are good at climbing and spend some time in trees. They also have excellent hearing and use many different sounds to talk to each other. Do you know what famous book has a dormouse as a character?

1. The Cat in the Hat
2. Math Is My Friend
3. Alice in Wonderland

Electric Eel

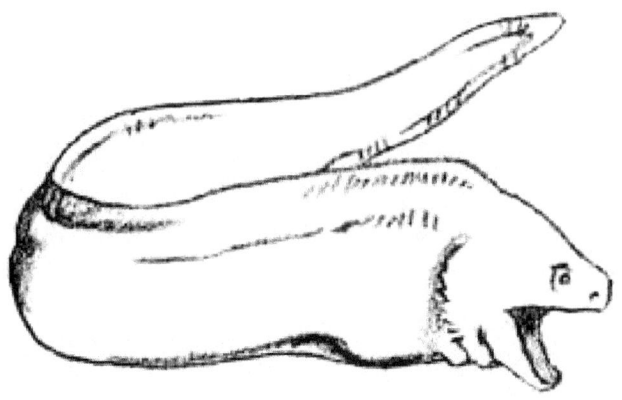

An eel is like a snake that lives in water, but electric eels are really not eels at all. They are fish. Electric eels are found in South American rivers. They really do have the ability to make electricity; so much that they can kill fish and small water animals to eat. Electric eels are colorful - dark grey on top with yellow-orange bellies. They can grow to be almost 6 feet long. Which part of an eel do you think makes the electricity?

1. The tail
2. The abdomen
3. The fingers

Ferret

Ferrets are domestic animals much like a weasels.
Farmers started using them 2500 years ago to
scare rabbits away from gardens. Nowadays
people keep them as pets. They are small and
usually brown, gray or black. Mice are their
favorite food. Sometimes you will find that
objects around the house disappear. This is
because ferrets hide them. Most ferrets sleep a lot,
up to 18 hours a day, but not all at once. They
sleep for a few hours and then get up to play.
Guess what game they love to play.

1. checkers
2. hide and seek
3. catch

Gibbon

Gibbons are apes that live in the jungles and rain forests of Asia, India, and Indonesia. They swing through the trees at a very fast speed. To do this they use their long arms, which are longer than their legs. They are faster than any other animal that travels that way. This is how they keep themselves safe. Gibbons eat all kinds of food, plants, fruit, insects, and little reptiles. They live as a family with a mother, father, and one baby. The families travel together in a troop. There is one thing that makes them different than a monkey. Do you know what it is?

1. They have no tail.
2. They live in the ocean.
3. They don't eat bananas.

Humpback Whale

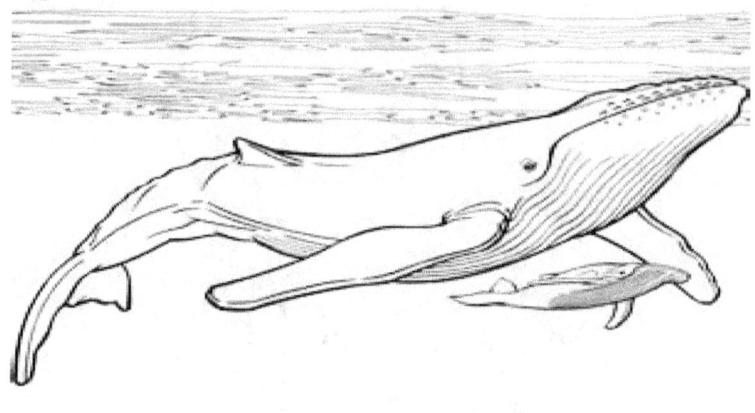

Humpback whales are known for being acrobatic. They like to do tricks like jump out of the water and splash back down. These whales live in two different places. In the summer they go north to the cold water around the Arctic Ocean. In the winter they go south to warmer water. They eat tiny fish called krill and plankton which they suck into their mouths. They eat during the winter and live all summer without eating. All whales have blow holes on top of their heads with which they blow out water when they breathe. But the humpback has more than one. Do you know how many?

1. two
2. four
3. one hundred

Impala

Impalas are a type of antelope and they live in the savannahs of Africa. The males have long horns that curve back over their bodies. The females do not have horns at all. One thing the impalas can do to escape from an enemy is to jump. Sometimes they can jump more than three feet off the ground. Impalas live in groups called herds and they travel around the grasslands eating grass and leaves. What do they use their horns for?

1. To hang their hat on
2. To get fruit from trees
3. To protect themselves

Jellyfish

A jellyfish is not really a fish. It is an animal that is not in any other group because it is not like any other animal on the planet. Its body has a jelly-like substance surrounded by skin and that's how it got its name. Most of its body is water. It also has long tentacles hanging down that feel and catch the fish that it eats. Jellyfish live all over the world in all the oceans. Some are dangerous because they have poison in their tentacles. Do you know what a jellyfish doesn't have in its body?

1. A mustache
2. Bones
3. Hair

Komodo Dragon

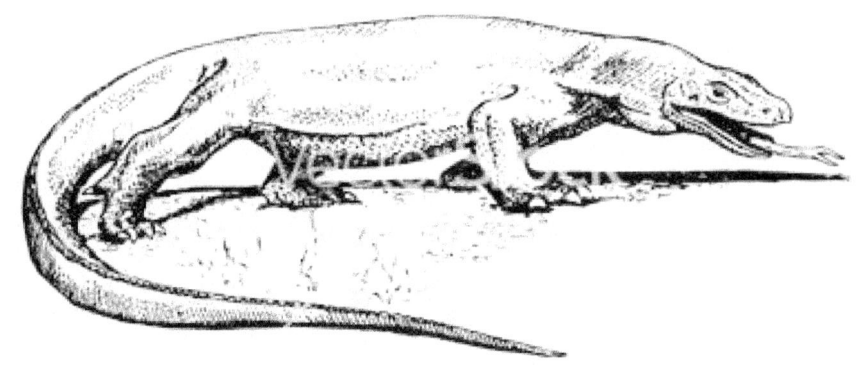

The Komodo dragon is not a dragon, but a huge lizard. They can grow to be nine feet long. They are very strong and attack their prey, sometimes animals that are bigger than they are. The dragons bite their prey and then follow them until they fall down. They have long, powerful tails which they use to prop themselves up with and stand on their hind legs. The Komodo lives only in Indonesia and is an endangered species. People didn't even know they existed until 100 years ago when a pilot crashed on their island. This giant lizard is very dangerous. Do you know why?

1. They are poisonous.
2. They run fast.
3. They throw knives at you.

Llama

Llamas are animals that grow a thick coat of wool. People keep them on farms and cut the wool to use to make clothing. They also use llamas as pack animals, which means they carry things on their backs. They have long necks that make them very tall, about 6 feet at the top of the head. Llamas are social and like to be around people. When they discipline their young, they spit at them.   One way they communicate with each other is by humming. You may think because they have wool coats that they are related to sheep. What animal are they more like?

1. camels
2. horses
3. sharks

Millipede

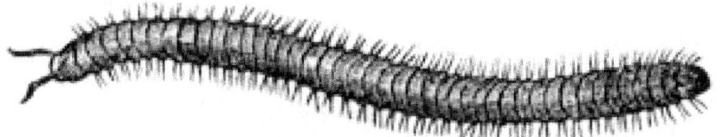

Even though the term "milli" means one thousand, these insects have only several hundred legs. There are many different kinds of millipedes. From tiny "ball bugs" to the African millipede which can be 14 inches long. Their legs are in groups on many body segments. They are rather slow moving and eat dried leaves, dead wood, fungi, and plant sap. You can find them in forests and under bushes all over the world.   Humans use millipedes in a special way. Do you know what it is?

1. as food
2. for paint brushes
3. To make medicine

Nightingale

These birds live in fields and forests in Europe. They build nests on the ground or in low bushes. In the winter they migrate to western Africa. Nightingales sing at night as well as during the day and their name actually means night songstress. They are so smart that they sing louder when they are in a town, so they can be heard over the traffic noise. A lot of poets use the nightingale as a symbol of sorrow because they think the bird's song sounds sad. This bird has been used in many stories, including one by Hans Christian Anderson. What is the nightingale most famous for?

1. Its beard
2. Its song
3. Its color

Oyster

Oysters are a kind of clam. People eat them, both cooked and raw. They also find pearls inside oysters and use them to make jewelry. And there is one kind of oyster that has a beautiful shiny shell that is used to make decorations. They live in the ocean in shallow water. Oysters grow all over the world, usually along the coast which makes them easy to harvest. They attach themselves to the floor of the ocean or to rocks along the shore. They have a two-part shell that they open and close as they need to eat. Hundreds of years ago lots of people ate oysters every day. What is a group of oysters called?

1. A bed
2. A flock
3. A train

Platypus

The platypus seems to be made up of many different animals. It has a body and fur like a mole, webbed feet like an otter, a tail like a beaver, and a duck's bill. Even though it is a mammal, it lays eggs. You may think it is cute, but the male has a sharp point on his back leg that spurts poison. The Platypus lives in rivers and streams. It eats shellfish, shrimp, worms and insects. It makes a home in a burrow along the riverbank. The platypus is found in only one country. Which one?

1. China
2. Moonopolis
3. Australia

Quail

Quail are small birds that live in many different environments all over the world. There are quail in desserts, woodlands, and rainforests. They have many different colors of feathers, but the most distinctive thing about them is a plume on the top of their heads. Quail eat insects, seeds, leaves, and grass. They make nests on the ground and you often see a mother with several chicks walking behind her. Quail have wings, but will run from danger before they try to fly away. People eat them like chicken and also enjoy quail eggs. What is a group of quail called?

1. A herd
2. A flock
3. A city

Rattlesnake

A rattlesnake is a poisonous reptile that lives in North America and South America. It has fangs that it uses to bite its prey and injects venom into the prey. The venom causes a lot of pain. The rattlesnake eats small animals like mice, rats, birds, and lizards. A rattlesnake has a tail that has hollow bones on the end which make the rattling sound when it senses an enemy. Its enemies include eagles, coyotes, foxes, weasels, owls, and humans. Like all snakes, it sheds its skin 2-3 times a year. The skin can feel different temperatures and often the snake lies in the sun to get warm. How does a rattlesnake get new rattles on its tail?

1. It glues them on.
2. It doesn't get new ones.
3. Another one grows when it sheds its skin.

Sea Otter

Sea Otters are weasel-like mammals that live in the ocean in the northern part of the world. They have the thickest fur of any mammal because they live in very cold water. They dive to the bottom of the ocean to get fish, clams, snails, and small shellfish. These otters have pouches under their front legs where food is stored until the animals get back to the surface. Then they use a rock to break open the shell of the food. When the otters aren't swimming, they often float on their backs, even when they sleep. Do you know what else they do when asleep?

1. Snore
2. Hold hands with their mate so they won't get separated
3. Dream about pickles

Tree Frog

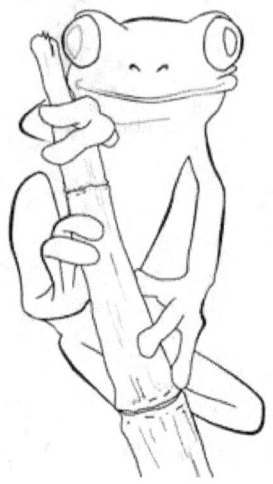

These little frogs really do live in trees. They are very small, no more than 4 inches long, and have joints in their legs and fingers along with discs on the end of the fingers that act like suction pads. This makes it easy for the frogs to grasp limbs and climb. There are many different kinds of tree frogs living in forests and jungles all over the planet. Some of the frogs make nests out of foam and set them on leaves. Some others make nests on the ground. The frogs eat insects and other bugs. One kind, the grey tree frog, can change its coloring just like another animal. Do you know which animal?

1. Chameleon
2. Snake
3. Elephant

Uakari

The uakari (its pronounced wa-ka-ri) is a small monkey that lives in hot jungles near water. It has long heavy fur all over its body except for the face. It has a very short tail compared to other monkeys. Uakari live in the rain forests around the Amazon River in South America. This animal stays in groups called troops that can have 10-30 members. Its food is mostly fruits along with leaves and insects and sometimes small animals. The face skin is a very different color than the fur. Can you guess what color?

1. White and black
2. Green stripes
3. Red or dark pink

Vulture

Vultures are large meat-eating birds that are scavengers. This means they wait for other animals to kill and feed on the prey and then they eat what is left over. They have extremely good eyesight and can see a dead animal when it is miles away. They live in many countries, usually in fields and in deserts. They start to fly in a circle in the air when they spot food. This action is called a kettle. A group that is feeding is called a _____.

1. Circle
2. Wake
3. Ballet

Wombat

Wombats live in Australia in fields, forests, and mountains. They are small with short legs and stubby tails. Their sharp teeth and claws let them dig burrows where they live underground. They stay close to their burrows because they are fat and move slowly. Wombats are herbivores and they eat grass, leaves, roots, and tree bark. People in Australia do not like wombats because they dig under fences and eat crops. The mother has one baby at a time. Do you know how she carries it?

1. in her teeth
2. in a backpack
3. in a pouch

X-ray Tetra

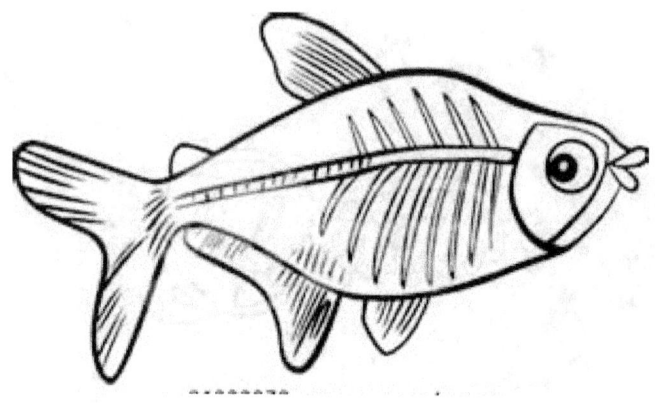

A tetra is a fish and this one is called the X-ray because its skin is so thin that it is transparent. It lives in large groups called schools. It can be found in South America along the coast at the mouth of the Amazon River. The x-ray tetra is sometimes known as the golden tetra because of the silvery-yellow color of its scales. It is one of the most popular freshwater fish to keep in an aquarium. This tetra also has a structure of bones inside its body that helps with which of its senses?

1. Sight
2. Hearing
3. Smell

Yak

Yaks are cow-like animals found in the mountains of central Asia. They have long hair that keeps them warm during the cold winters. A herd of yaks has mostly female members. Yaks eat grass, leaves, and herbs, spending their days in the meadows. And like cows, they have four stomachs. All yaks have long horns that they use in the winter to dig under the snow to find food. They are gentle and easily trained. Humans use them for pulling carts and carrying heavy loads. Another thing humans do with yaks is use them in a sport. Which one do you think it is?

1. Racing
2. Sledding
3. Basketball

Zebu

Another Asian cow-like animal is the zebu. They live in the southern parts of the continent where it is hot. In fact, they are the only kind of cattle to be able to live in tropical jungles. They have long curved horns, a humps on their backs, and droopy ears. Zebu are used as pack animals and to pull carts on farms. They are also used as dairy and beef cattle. In India they are known as Brahmin and are protected for religious reasons. The zebu has a large flap of skin under the jaw. Can you guess what it is called?

1. A throat
2. A pillow
3. A dewlap

ANSWERS

Aardvark   1) It runs in a zig-zag.

Bison   3) A nickel

Cassowary   1) soil (dirt)

Dormouse   3) Alice in Wonderland

Electric Eel   2) The abdomen

Ferret   2) Hide and seek

Gibbon   1) It has no tail.

Humpback Whale   1) Two

Impala   3) To protect themselves

Jellyfish   2) Bones

Komodo Dragon   1) They are poisonous.

Llama 1) Camels

Millipede   3) To make medicine

Nightingale   2) Its song

Oyster   1) A bed

Platypus   3) Australia

Quail   2) A flock

Rattlesnake   3) When it sheds its skin

Sea Otter   2) They hold hands with their mates.

Tree Frog   1) Chameleon

Uakari   2)Rred or dark pink

Vulture   2) A wake

Wombat   3) In her pouch

X-ray Tetra   2) Hearing

Yak   1) Racing

Zebu   3) A dewlap

The next book in this series will be

Trivia For Kids: Food

Other books by Elizabeth Gross

Word Love: The Rise and Fall of a Blog

Internet History Trivia

available on Amazon